The Sparrow and I
Mean Mary
with Frank James

Photography by Johnny Giles

Music Engraving and Layout by Charylu Roberts

Transcribed by Mary James (banjo) and Frank James (guitar)

Special thanks to Jean James and Jim Brown

13097 Highway 45 N, Finger, TN 38334
www.woodrockhouse.com

Copyright © 2011 WoodRock House

All rights reserved. No part of this book may be reproduced or copied
in any form without the written permission of the publisher.

"The piano may do for love-sick girls who lace themselves to skeletons, and lunch on chalk, pickles and slate pencils. But give me the banjo."
~Mark Twain

www.meanmary.com

Table of Contents

Introduction 4

Mean Mary's Story 5

Banjo Annotations 8

SONGS:

Good Time Gal 9

I've Been Down 15

The Sparrow and the Hawk** 20

Sugar Creek Mountain* 27

Memphis Moon* 30

Dance of the Thistledown 34

Joy 39

Sparrow Alone* 44

All songs written by Mary James
*Co-written by Jean James
**Co-written by Frank James

Introduction I

Let me start by saying that this project definitely brought out a lot of emotions in me … primarily the "Why on earth did I think this was a good idea?" emotion. There was also the "Oh my gosh, I'm never going to finish this!" emotion, followed by the "If you play it one more time that way, I'm going to kill you, Frank!" emotion, and finally … the "I'm so glad I did this … you're a wonderful brother!" emotion. (Okay, the "wonderful brother" part might be pushing it a bit.)

Some of these songs are older tunes of mine that I've been playing for a few years, while songs, like "The Sparrow and the Hawk," we were still writing the day we videoed it. In fact, a week or so after we had finished that song, I decided I would like to play it at a show with Frank. As it turned out, parts of the song had already become a complete and utter fog in our over-musiced brains—thank heavens we had our trusty tablature book! So, at the very least, "The Sparrow and the Hawk" has already gotten thorough use by its authors.

I hope you have as much fun with this book as I'm having, now that I'm not working on it anymore! :) Rather than leave you with my own meager words of wisdom, I'll leave you with this quote from my favorite composer:

> *"Then let us all do what is right, strive with all our might toward the unattainable, develop as fully as we can the gifts God has given us, and never stop learning."*
>
> ~Ludwig Beethoven

Love,
Mary

Introduction II

When Mary originally commissioned *Yours Truly* to contribute to this book, the concept was considerably different from what you have before you. The title was to be *The Sparrow and the Dodo: Psychedelic Guitar Arrangements Only Frank Can Comprehend, with Some Banjo, Courtesy of Frank's Sister*. However, being the humble soul that I am, I decided it would be best if I stayed within my capabilities. Utilizing my uncanny knack for knowing just how little-as-possible I can get away with, I present to you these, my efforts, for your amusement.

Best Personal Regards,
Frank James

Mean Mary's Story

Gypsy Girl:

"Mean" Mary James, youngest of six children, was born in Geneva, Alabama, though her family lived in Florida, a couple miles below the Alabama line. Her mom (author, Jean James) and dad (WWII veteran, William James) lived a very nomadic lifestyle. On one occasion they packed up the family (Mary was four at the time) and moved from Florida to North Minnesota, near the Canadian border, to rough it in the wilds.

The North Country:

For three months they lived in a tent built from a roll of Visqueen they'd brought with them. During this time, they built a log cabin using only an axe, hand saws, and the trees around them. They cooked their food on a campfire, got their water from a deep hole they'd dug, and read at night by the northern lights shining through the clear walls of their plastic tent. On one occasion their tent was mauled by a large, 7"1" black bear that Mary's mom, Jean, was forced to shoot.

The tent soon became unbearably cold, and when they finally moved into their almost completed log cabin, winter was upon them. Without electricity or running water, and cold enough to freeze water five feet from the only source of heat (an old wood stove), the family spent many hours reading books by kerosene lamp and enjoying the great outdoors (cutting firewood!).

First Guitar:

Mary's oldest brother, Jim, who'd just joined the Navy, sent the family a guitar and a compilation tape of songs he liked. With a battery-powered tape-player, the family listened to the music of Hank Williams, Jr. and Dolly Parton. It wasn't long before Mary was singing the songs plus vocalizing all the instrumentation. Seeing her talent, Mom and Dad bought guitar books, and Mom started teaching all the children how to play the guitar. Mary and her brother Frank were the two who would turn music into a career.

Mary learned to read music before she could read words and was an official singer/songwriter before she'd started her first day of kindergarten. With the help of her mom, she wrote her theme song "Mean Mary from Alabam'." The press immediately baptized her with this handle, and she's been Mean Mary ever since.

Goodness, Snakes Alive:

The James family eventually migrated back to Florida. Mary's dad (who was sixty when she was born) was now retired, and Mary's mom searched for ways to help support the family as well as feed Mary's musical appetite and the varied interests of their other children. She started an organic truck farm, built and sold live-animal traps, collected live reptiles, amphibians, and mammals for wholesale distributors, and collected live venomous snakes for antivenom production. The children joined in all these undertakings and found it great sport.

On the Road Again:

Mary was now playing guitar, banjo, and fiddle. She recorded her first album at age six and spent five hours a day on instrumental and vocal practice along with her live performances. When she upped her music study time to seven hours a day, and her road shows began to multiply, it became impossible for her to attend school. At the end of the second grade, she went into home study and also started appearing daily on the *Country Boy Eddie Show*, a regional TV program out of Birmingham, Alabama. During this time, she also appeared regularly in Nashville, Tennessee at the Nashville Palace, on the Nashville Network, the Elvis Presley Museum, and on Printer's Alley.

In spite of her hectic schedule, she found time for her studies and when only nine years old, she aced a state required test at a twelfth grade equivalency level. This wasn't surprising to her parents who had witnessed her read the entire *Gone with the Wind* novel at age seven.

Her guitarist brother, Frank James, who'd now joined her on stage and in the home school program, also excelled in his studies and at age fourteen taught himself trigonometry. He graduated from high school at fifteen.

Back in Time:

At one point, Mary and Frank were booked at a living history event. They immediately fell in love with folk music. They'd grown weary of the commercial, country-music scene and started a tour of historic folk and Civil War era music. It wasn't long before they were one of the most sought after historical folk groups in the country, being booked every weekend and having to turn down hundreds of shows a year.

There was only one problem with this new arena of music to Mary's fourteen-year-old eyes: all those mounted reenactors riding around while she stood in the dust and played music. Mary had always wanted a horse, and being a wise teenager, she slyly told her parents that the only reason she'd worked so hard on music was so she could one day afford one! When her brother, Frank, who was equally drawn by equestrian interests, seconded her resolve, Mom and Dad gave in.

Horsing Around:

Always creative with new ideas to make money for her kids' dreams, Mom started selling fudge at their live shows. The revenues from this enterprise almost too quickly materialized into horse flesh: an Arabian mix which Frank named Rogue, and a green-broke Thoroughbred mix which Mary named Apache. They promptly added "horse-back music" to their overflowing repertoire and began playing "mounted" music whenever they could book it. This led them from parades to wild-west shows and even a few bank robberies (re-enacted, of course).

Apache was a spirited horse and constantly got into trouble. He loved to perform, but that didn't stop his proclivity for accidents. He once reared in a parade and fell over backwards on Mary and her guitar. Another time, when spooked by a deer, he bolted, his saddle broke, Mary fell underneath, and was trampled by his running hooves. He also, at times, liked to roll down hills with Mary astride. But in spite of broken bones, swollen limbs, twisted legs, and multiple bruises, Mary never missed a show, though she did on occasion have to prop herself against a support.

California, Here They Come:

In the meantime, Mary and Frank were eliciting interest from a California music agency, and Mom James had just signed a contract with a California literary agency. The other children were all grown and on their own by this time, so Mom, Dad, Frank, and Mary did the "Beverly Hillbilly" thing. They packed all their belongings into, and onto, their vehicles, hooked up the horse trailer with Rogue and Apache, and drove to LA.

For the next three years, Mary and Frank were involved in almost every TV show and movie produced in the Hollywood area—be it as background actor, stand-in, photo double, stunt double, or day player. Mary found a large, beat-up, slide-in camper for the back of her pickup truck that cost only two hundred dollars, and that became her home. She parked it wherever it was convenient, and sometimes in places not so convenient. There are, no doubt, still dents on low-hanging limbs all over the LA area, thanks to Mary and her top-heavy home. And then there was the time she took the mirror off a movie executive's car at Fox studios by trying to squeeze through an impossibly-narrow area. She bought him a new mirror but never got a movie roll out of the happening!

It was exciting, interesting work, but it wasn't furthering her music career, and the horses didn't like it at all. They longed for the green fields they were used to. Eventually the James Gang migrated back to the South, finding homes in Tennessee.

The Great Setback:

The horses were happy, and Mary's music career was really taking off, when the most devastating event of her life occurred. One rainy evening in February she was the front-seat passenger in a small car when the driver lost control. Mary's head broke the windshield, and her neck cracked the hard plastic dashboard. The twisted state of her neck convinced the driver she was gone. He even called her parents and told them she was dead. But a high-speed ambulance ride and quick medical attention at the hospital saved her life, if not her future. It was there she received news that, to her, was worse than death—her right vocal cord was paralyzed.

She brought her battered body home from the hospital and began her fight. Music was her life—had always been her life—and she couldn't give it up. She purposely set herself to do the hardest of physical tasks, demanding that her body get well. She stacked hay bales, built fences and barns, took winter swims, and constantly worked her vocal cords. The rest of her body soon recovered from the trauma, but her right vocal cord stayed paralyzed. The left side tried to compensate for it, making it possible for her to sing a little, but only for about ten minutes at a time, and her voice was dead next to its former capabilities.

A Bit of Light in the Darkness:

One joyous day, six months later, a throat specialist told her there was slight movement in her frozen vocal cord. He said it might not totally recover, might not even improve further, but his news was enough for Mary. That was when her real work began. She booked shows, sang when she could, and when she couldn't, she'd play her instruments.

She started touring again, sometimes alone, sometimes with her brother, and sometimes with her full band. She also got her own Nashville TV show: *The Never-Ending Street*, a documentary/reality type of show depicting the trials and joys of a touring musician.

During this time, she co-wrote novels with her mom. To date, one novel is with a publisher and is available at bookstores: *Sparrow Alone on the Housetop*. Another four novels are with an agent along with a devotional book she co-wrote with her mom and Frank.

It was also during this same time that her YouTube videos began to take off. They'd started out with a few daily visits but quickly climbed to over four thousand visits a day. Her bookings increased and her international fan base took a leap of growth. This was all good news, but the greatest thing to happen during this time was the recovery of her vocal cord. She'd worked it back to life!

On the Never-Ending Street:

Today she labors on her TV show, produces music for herself and other artists, produces shows and videos, is co-writing a novel trilogy about the music world, is an endorsing artist for Deering Banjos, and is constantly touring. She plays 11 instruments and has recorded 12 albums, her newest being *Walk a Little Ways with Me*.

There is not room here to tell the whole life story of Mean Mary, but if you'd like to hear more of it, listen to her music—it's all there.

Banjo Annotations
by Mary James

Firstly, let me confess that I never play one of my songs the same way twice in a row. The changes are sometimes subtle, but even on the DVD you might notice a difference between the performed version and the practice version. I did make sure the tablature perfectly coincides with the practice version … well, almost perfectly! :)

Secondly, my fingerpicking methods are borderline crazy. My thumb is my dominant picker, and you might notice I give it a good work out in these songs. I like to use the thumb to emphasize notes, and the index and middle finger don't quite give the same punch. The right-hand fingering positions on these songs are written the way I play them. If they don't work for you, please do what's comfortable or what feels right.

Thirdly, all of these songs are in open G tuning. "I've Been Down," "The Sparrow and the Hawk," and "Dance of the Thistledown" are capoed to A (capo at second fret). The fifth string should either be capoed to A or tuned up to an A note.

Lastly, but not leastly, make these songs your own. These might be my songs and my arrangements, but when you're playing them, they're all yours. Embellish, delete, change the rhythm, play sad, play slow, play happy, play fast, just play what you feel and never be hindered by any pre-conceived notion that there is a right way and a wrong way to make music.

For additional tips visit *www.yearofthesparrow.com*

The arrangement of this bluegrass/jazz tune can definitely keep you on your toes, rhythmically. At the start of section A3, the rhythm really takes on a new feel. Bars 70-75 have an arrow that indicates an upstroke with the thumb.

Good Time Gal

Written by "MEAN" MARY JAMES

Key: G

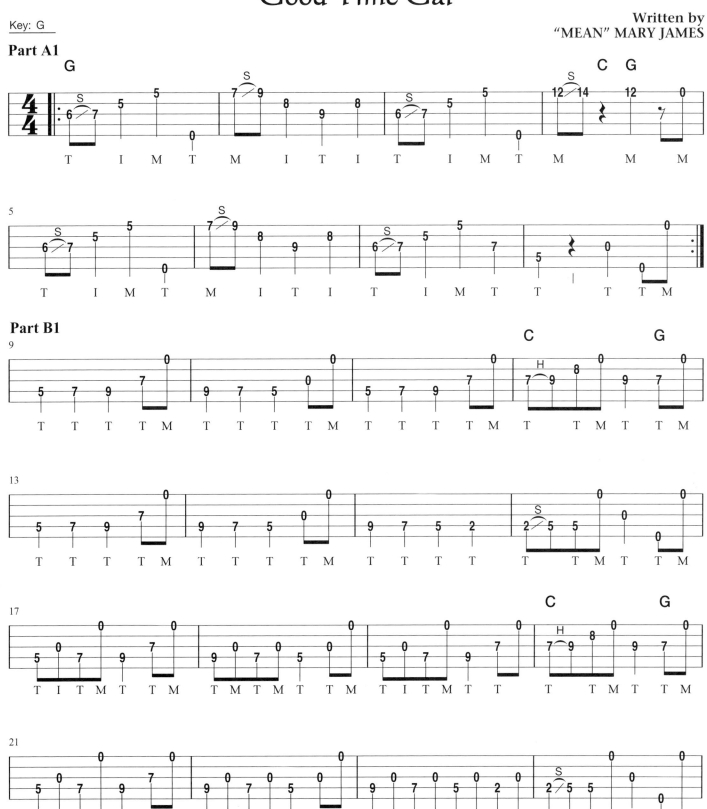

Copyright © 2011 by Mary James
All Rights Reserved   Used by Permission

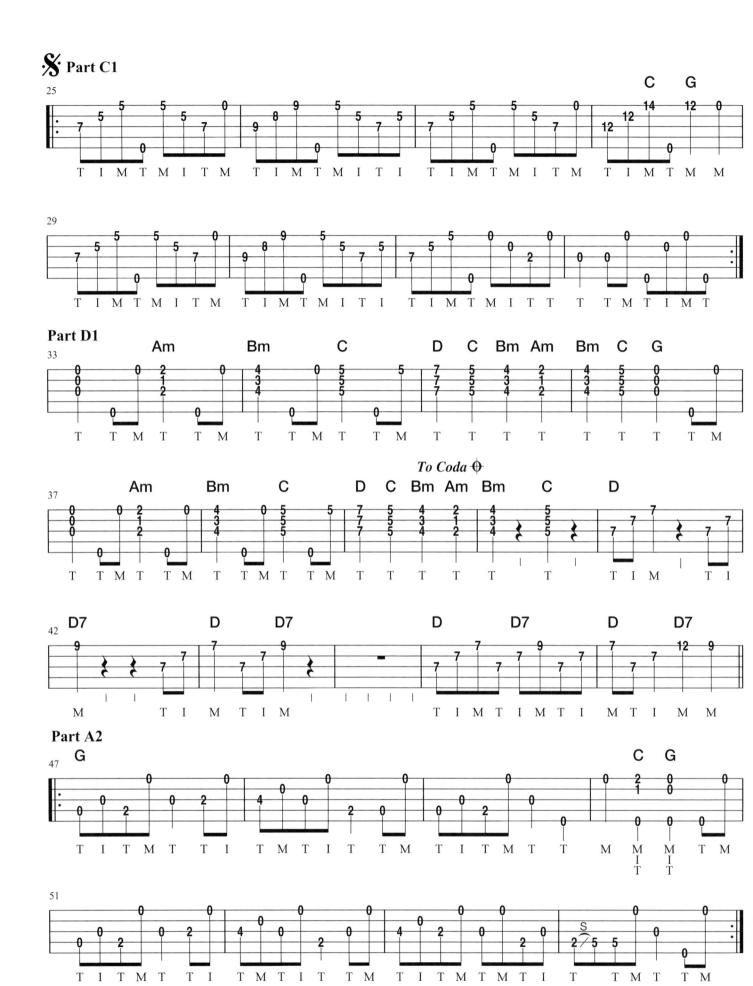

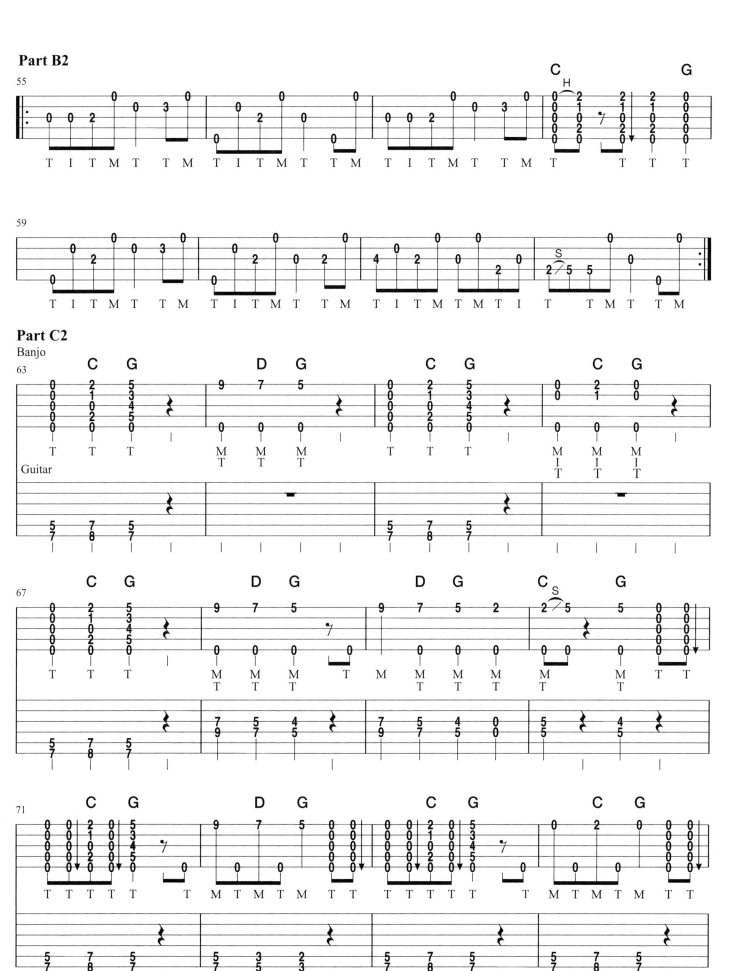

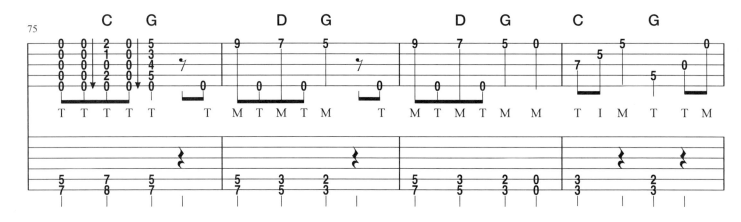

Part D2

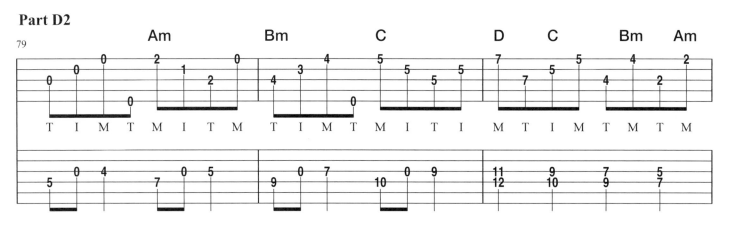

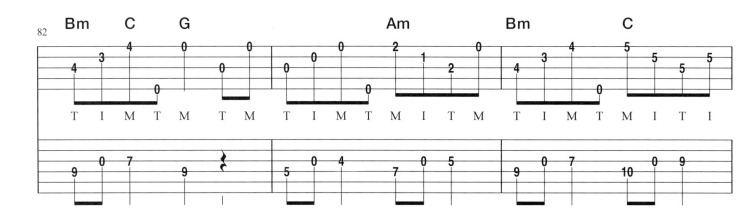

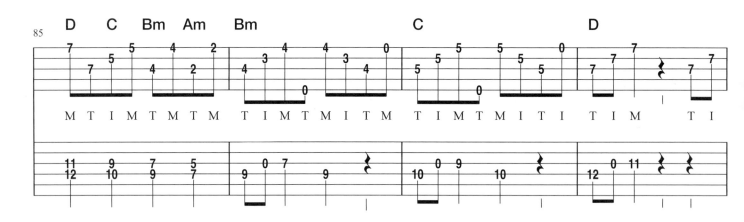

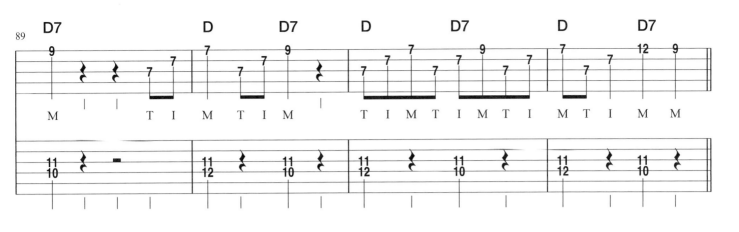

Part A3

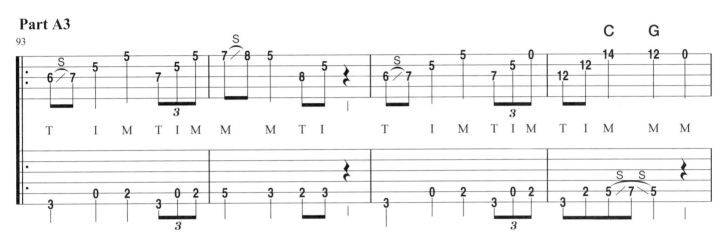

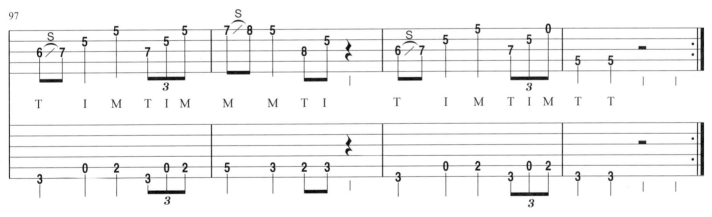

Part B3

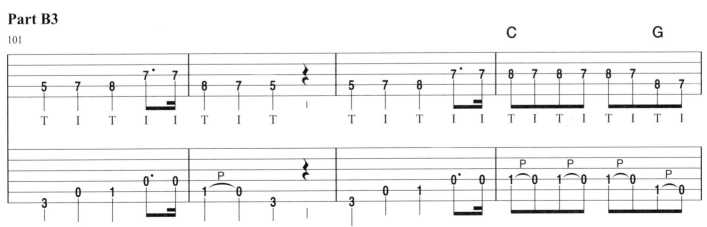

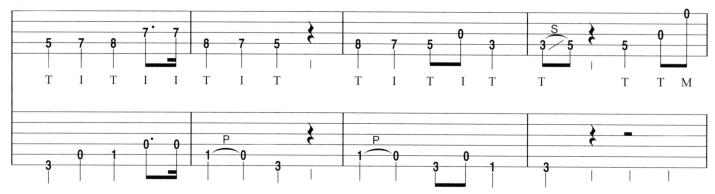

Guitar returns
to playing chords

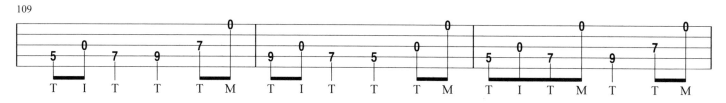

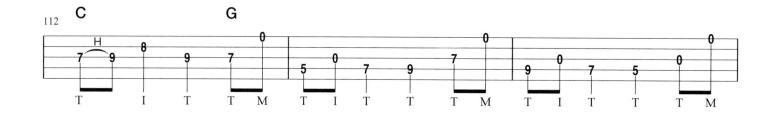

D.S. % al Coda
*Pause before banjo comes
back in at Part C1*

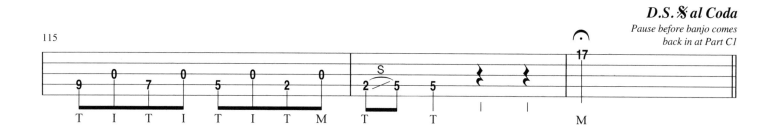

⊕ *Coda*

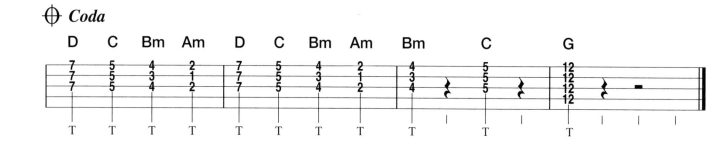

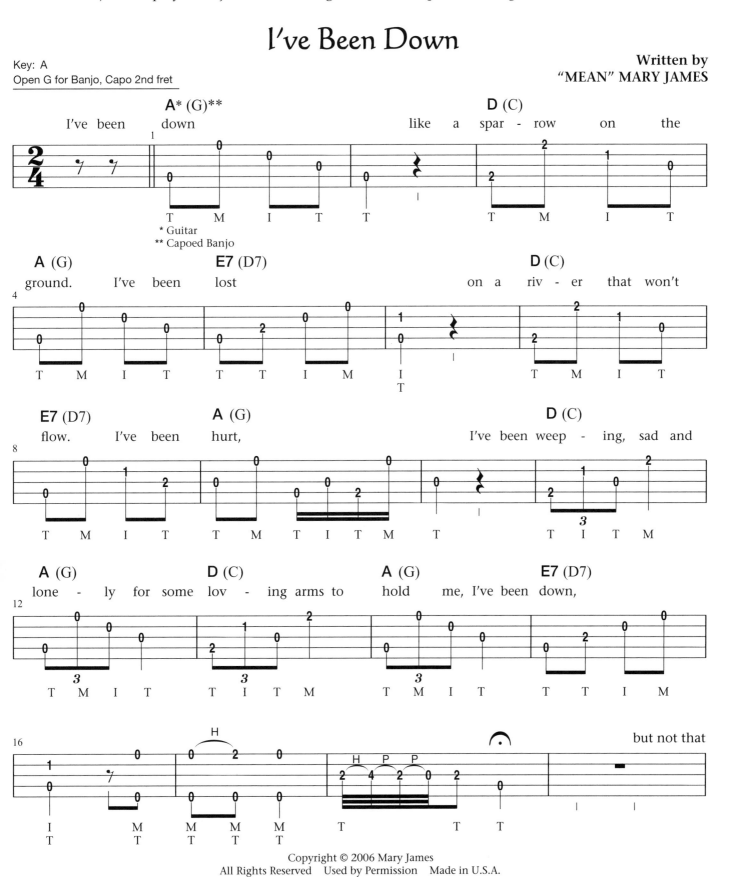

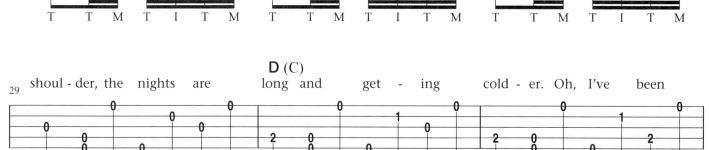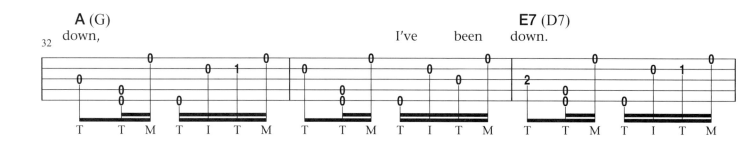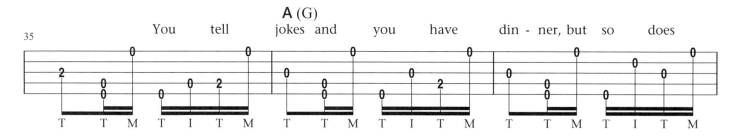

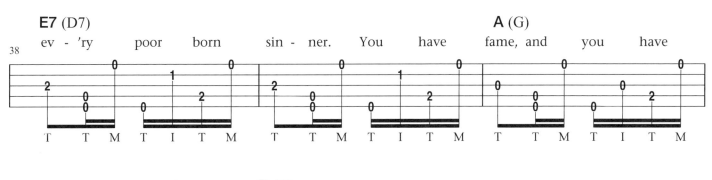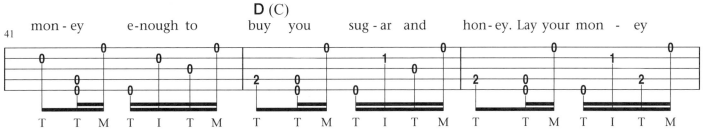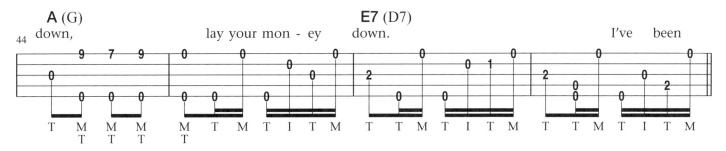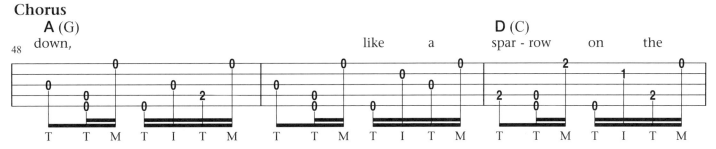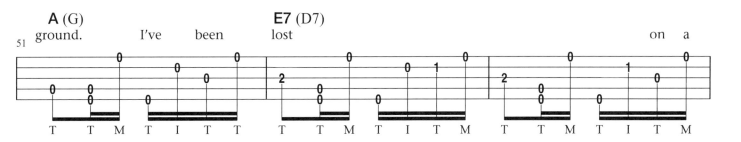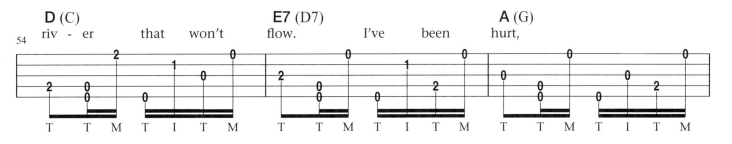

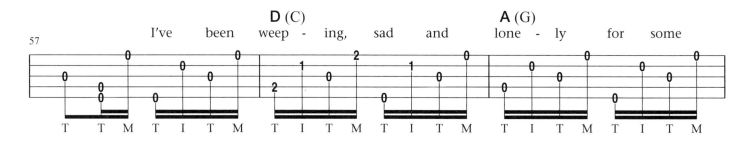
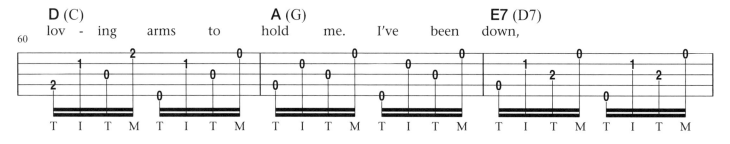
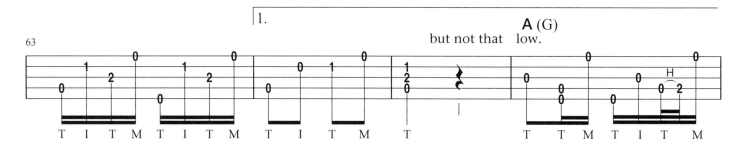
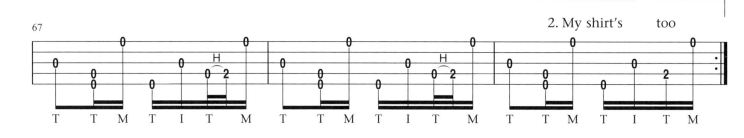
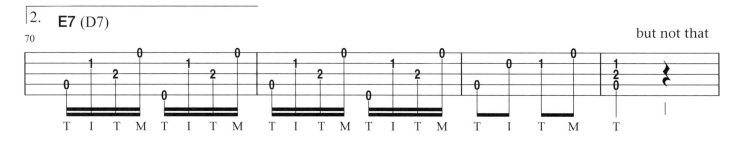
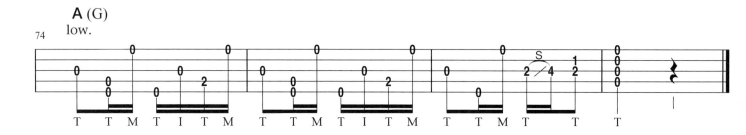

Additional Lyrics

2. My shirt's too big, my boots are battered,
   my skirt's too long, it's worn and tattered.
   I ain't got no fine clothes for Sunday,
   and I'll look just as poor on Monday;
   I've been down, I've been down.

   You have everything folks desire,
   you have anyone you want for hire.
   So you think I will wear your red gown
   if you lay your money down, lay your money down.
   Chorus

Mary at age seven, Frank at age eleven

This is a banjo and guitar duet with a classical feel. It is very important the banjo and guitar work together in this song. As banjo players, we're used to playing rolls to fill up space in a song. Think the opposite in this song. Enjoy the sound of your notes, sustaining through the pauses, and keep the waltz timing in your head. The rhythm change from bar 124 to 125 will probably take a little getting used to; again, the banjo and guitar need to work together to make it flow.

The Sparrow and the Hawk

Key: D
Open G for Banjo, Capo 2nd fret

Written by
"MEAN" MARY JAMES
and FRANK JAMES

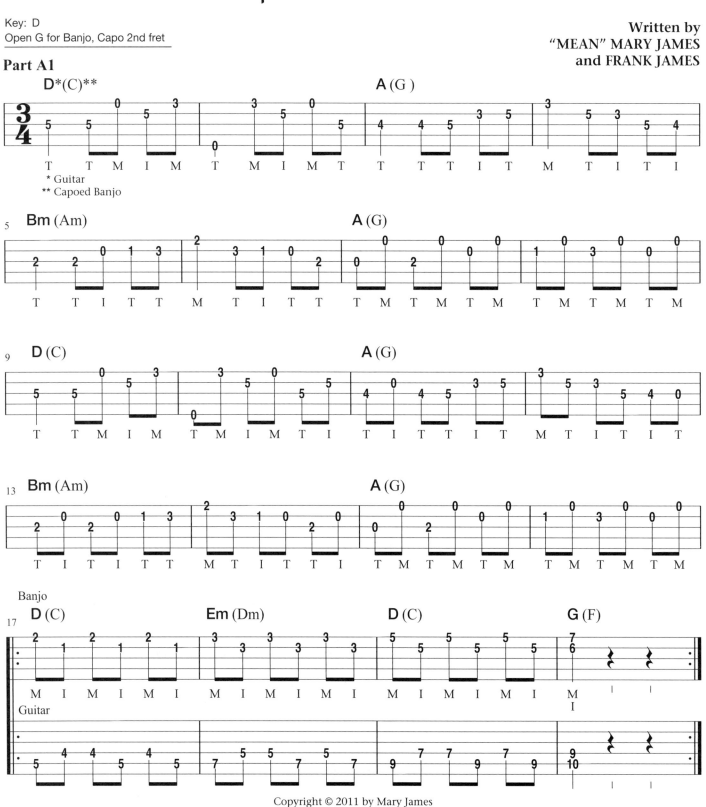

* Guitar
** Capoed Banjo

Copyright © 2011 by Mary James
All Rights Reserved   Used by Permission

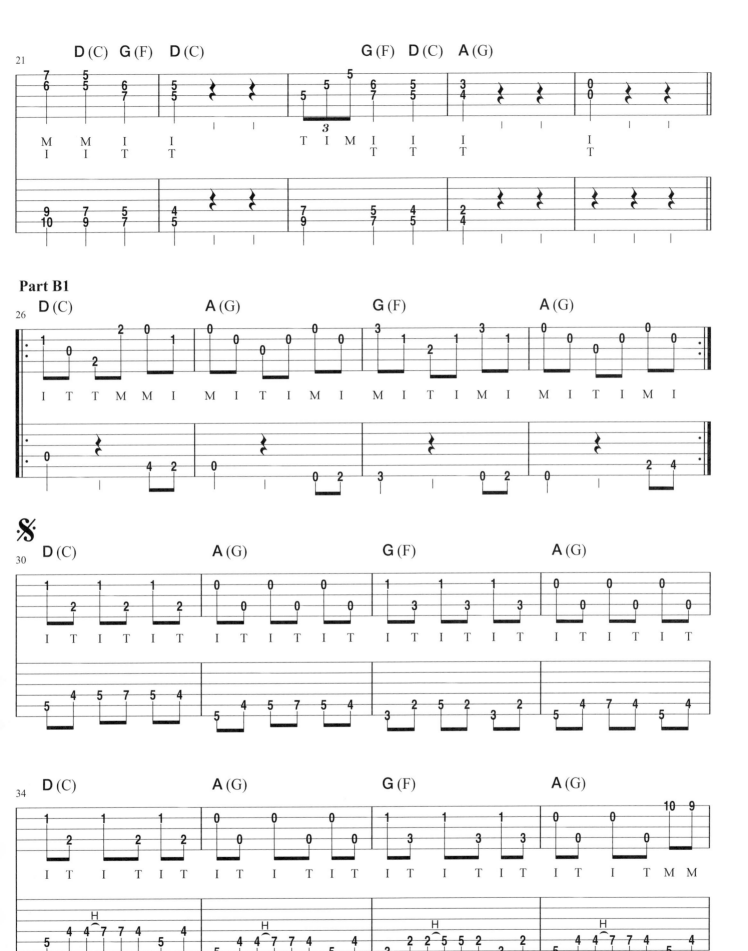

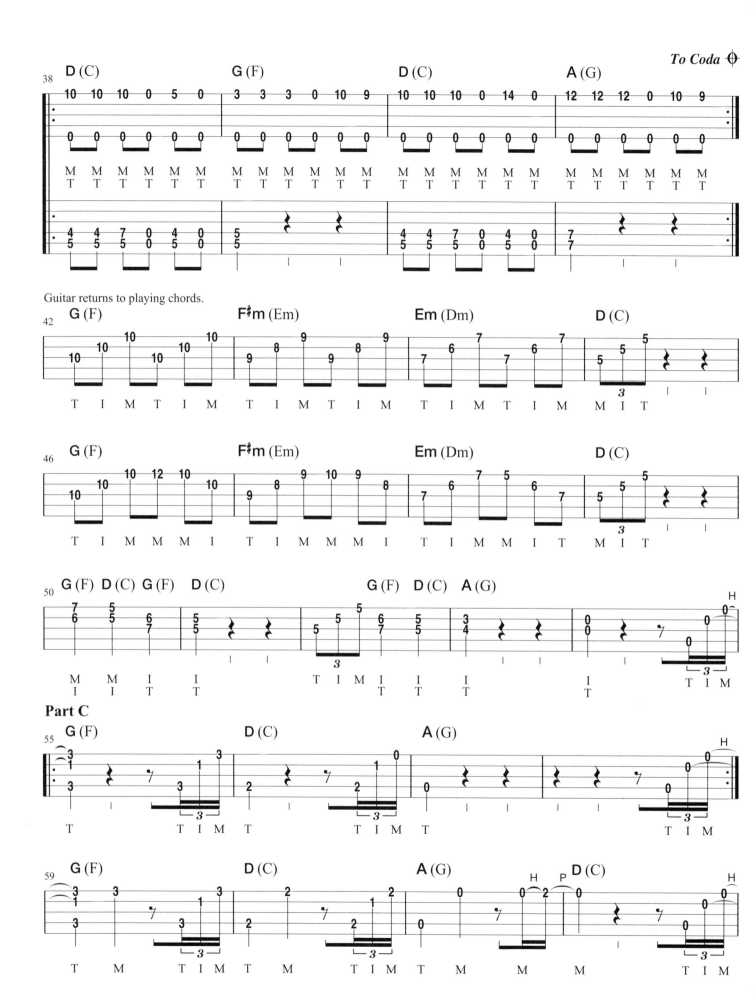

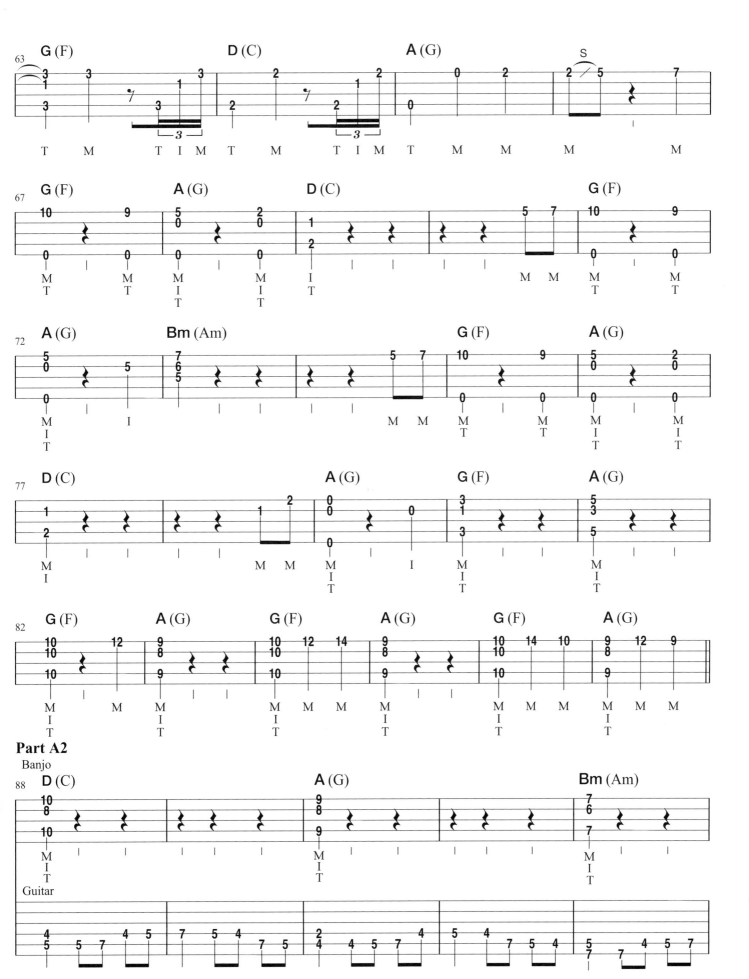

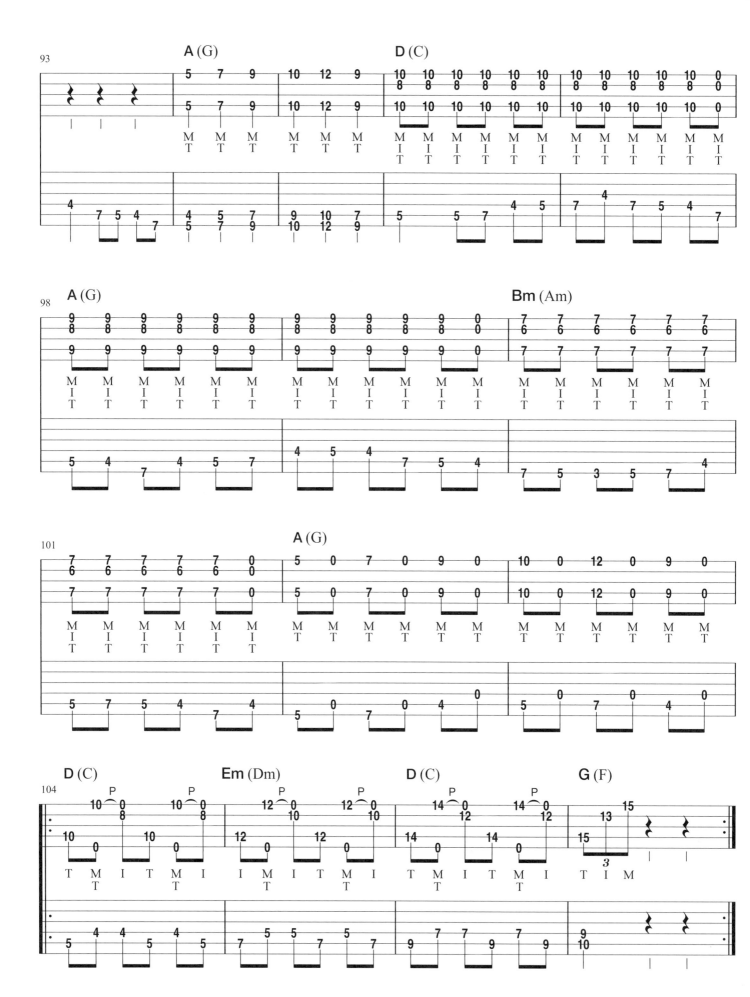

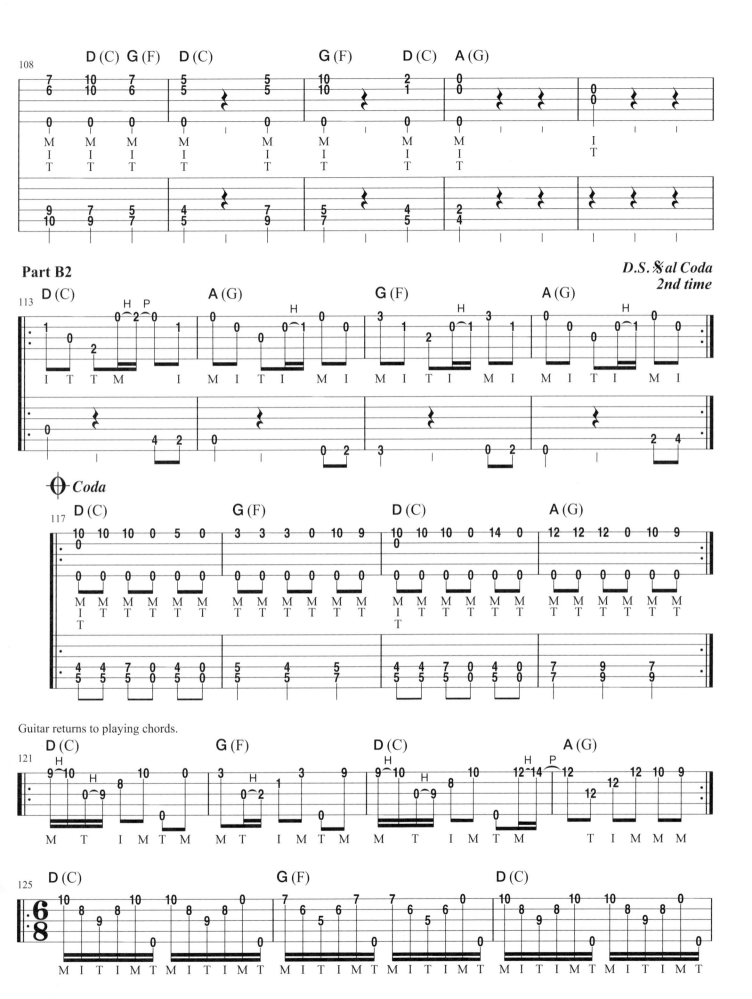

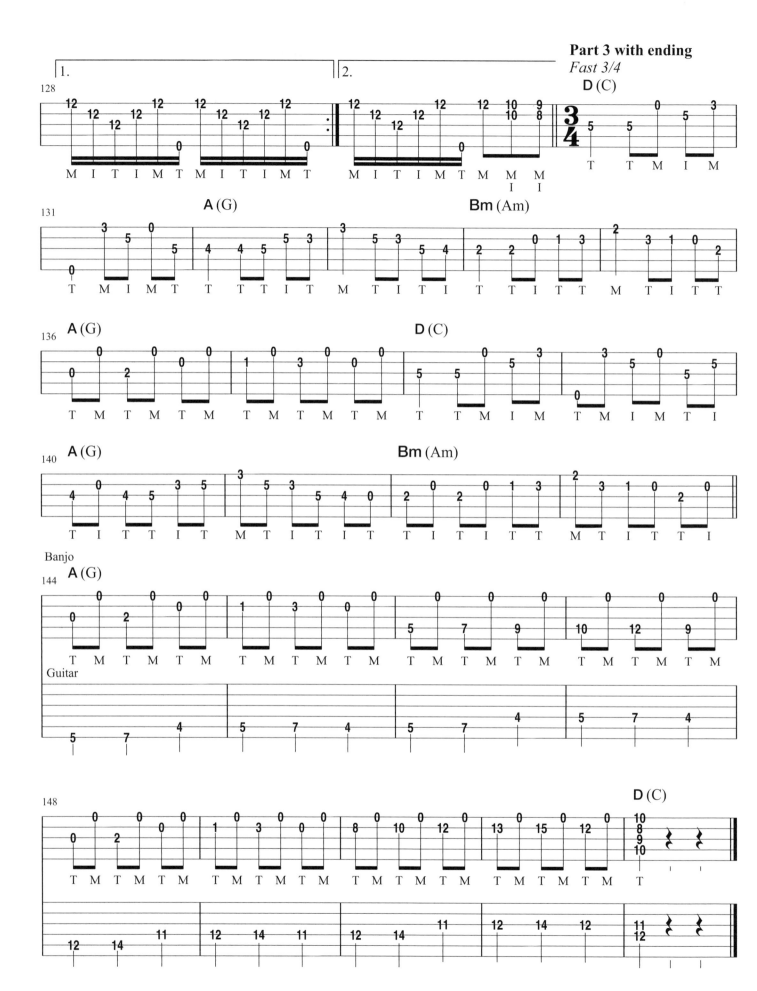

Not a whole lot to say about this song—it's just your traditional, bluegrass tune. Everything is pretty basic, and it's a good song to learn if you're a beginner.

Sugar Creek Mountain

Written by
"MEAN" MARY JAMES
and JEAN JAMES

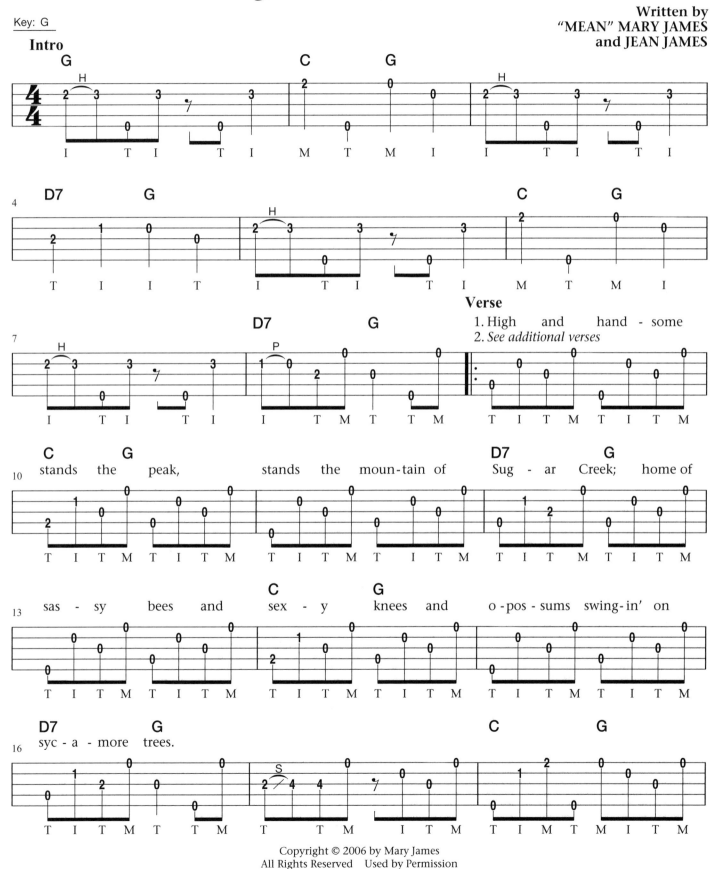

Copyright © 2006 by Mary James
All Rights Reserved   Used by Permission

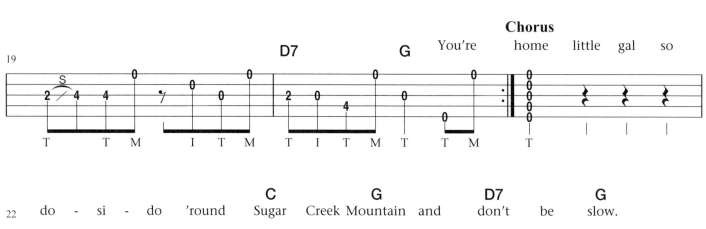
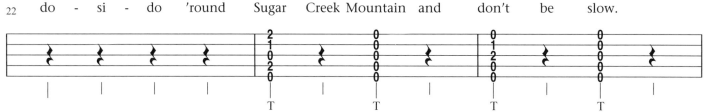
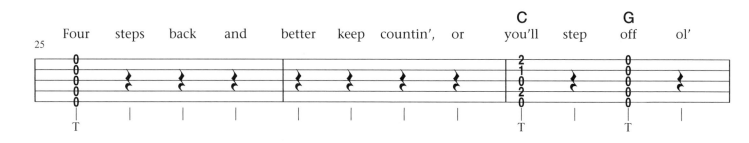
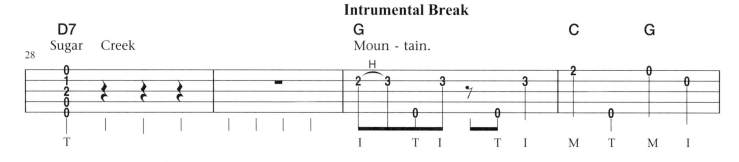
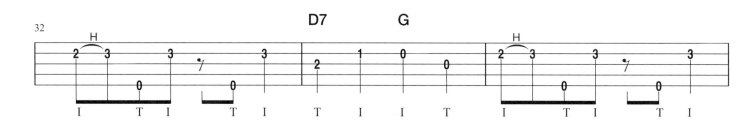
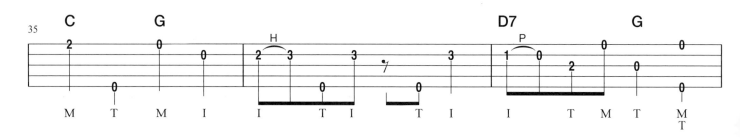

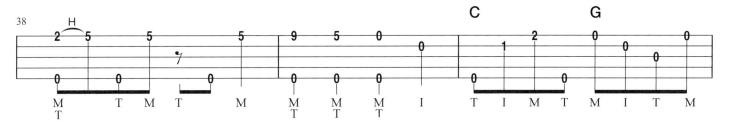
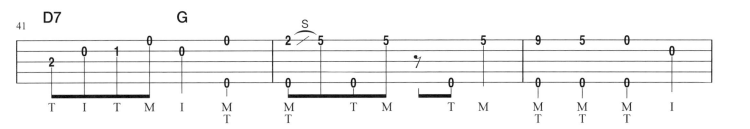
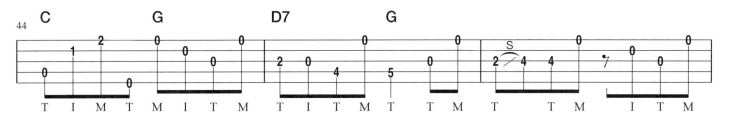
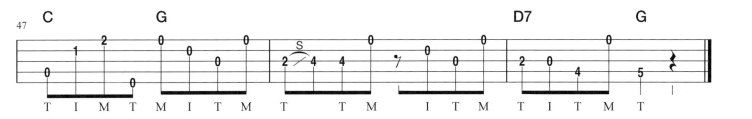

Additional Lyrics

2. You can sit and stare at nothin' in particular,
   sit and dream where life's perpendicular;
   sky and trees and rocks and ground,
   all up and down and all around.
   Chorus: You're home little gal …

3. Wait for the wisdom that wind will bring,
   learn how to live and love and sing,
   breathe in deep and feel the burnin',
   deeper than life and deeper than learnin'.

4. Wild sweet notes from a wild sweet throat
   echoing songs that never been wrote.
   Wild and sweet like a sugar cane treat,
   dance the fellas right off their feet
   Chorus: You're home little gal …

Chorus 2. With feet a prancin' and yo' blood a dancing,
   eyes a glancin' while yo' heart's romancin',
   swing to the music of that clear sweet fountain
   that slides down the side of Sugar Creek Mountain.

5. You can't get to heaven if you push and shove,
   just promenade the one you love.
   Oh by Joe, and oh by gee,
   don't look at her when you dance with me.

6. Dive through the middle, don't shove or push,
   keep goin' round the mulberry bush.
   Oh by gosh, and oh by Joe,
   this may be the last time, I don't know.
   Chorus: You're home little gal …

Feel the blues. This is another song where the banjo is more of a back-up to the vocal. In order to get the best feel on the rhythm count, definitely listen to this song while you read the tablature. The whole song is picked with just the thumb and index finger. Bars 13-16 have a deadening effect that is best explained on the DVD.

Memphis Moon

Written by
"MEAN" MARY JAMES
and JEAN JAMES

Key: Cm

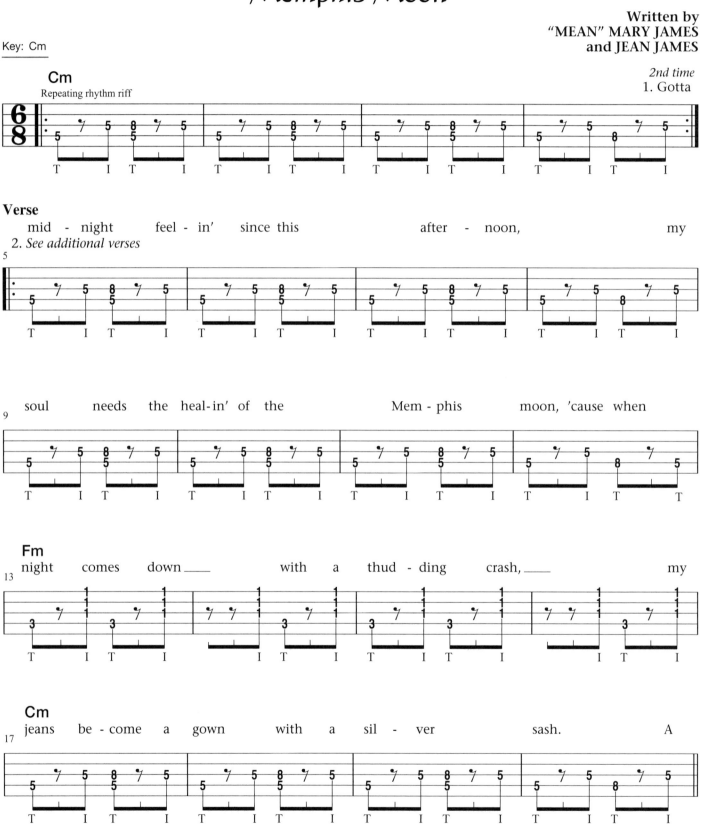

Copyright © 2011 by Mary James
All Rights Reserved   Used by Permission

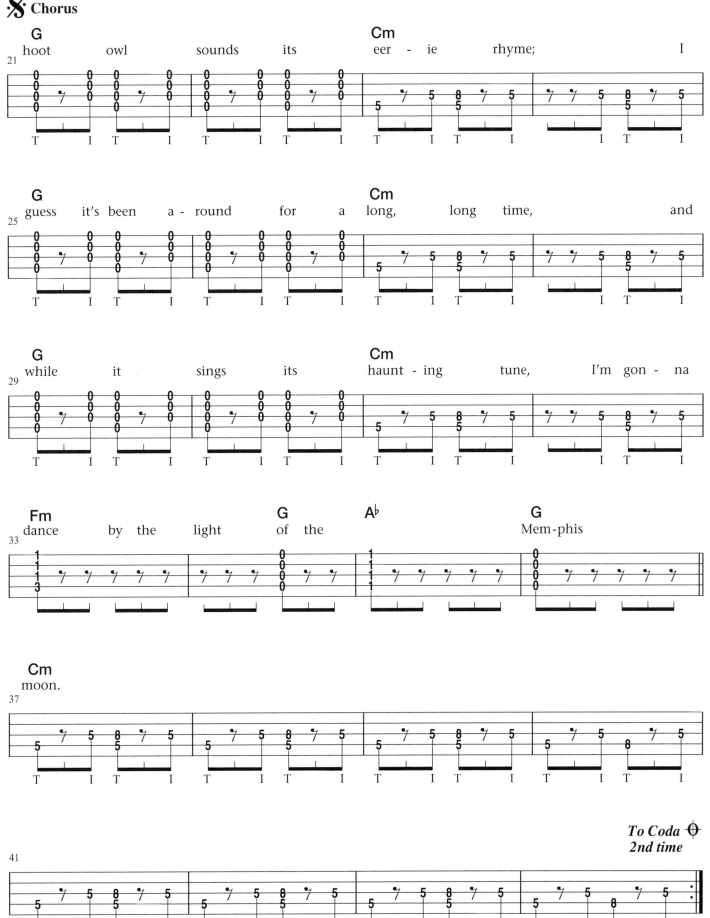

Instrumental

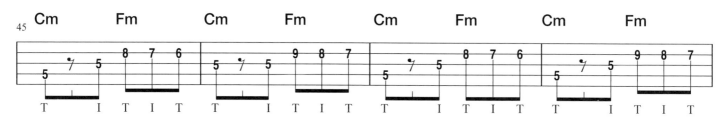

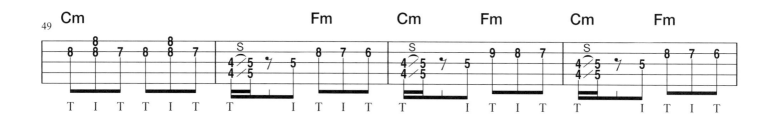

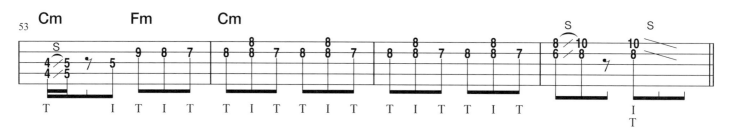

Bridge

Time danc - es slow to the rhy - thm of my feet; the

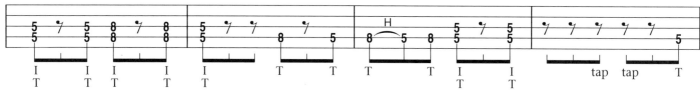

moon hangs low o - ver Be - ale Stre -

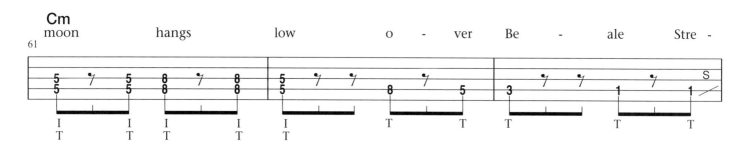

D.S. % al Coda
(Repeat Chorus)

et.

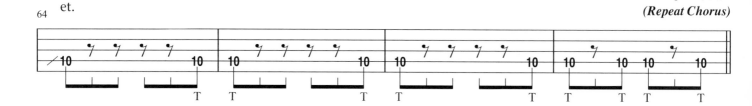

Coda

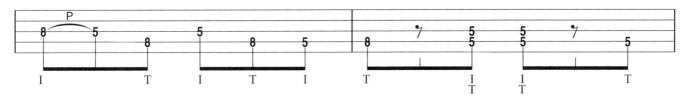

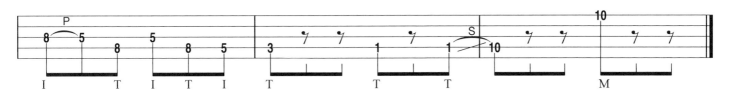

Additional Lyrics

Verse 2. Dark waters swell to a river boat's cry,
the stars all yell and the willows sigh.
Deep as death, the Mighty Mississip'
just rolls along like she's takin' a trip.

Chorus 2. Making her rounds in her muddy shoes,
dressing in browns but singin' in blues.
Midnight fever's bound to hit me soon,
I'm gonna dance by the light of the ... Memphis moon.

This is a Celtic tune that sounds best when you have another instrument playing a strong back-up. In section C, there's a tricky change in the rhythm feel that might take a little getting used to.

Dance of the Thistledown

Key: A
Open G for Banjo, Capo 2nd fret

Written by
"MEAN" MARY JAMES

Part A1

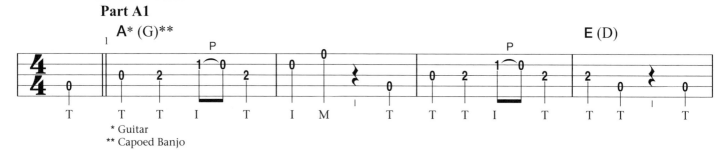

* Guitar
** Capoed Banjo

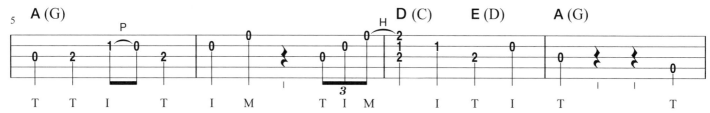

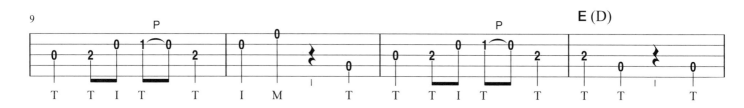

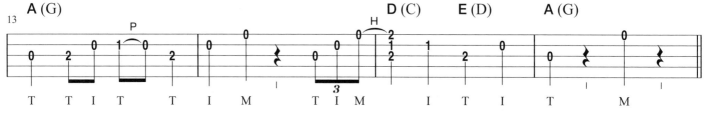

Part B1

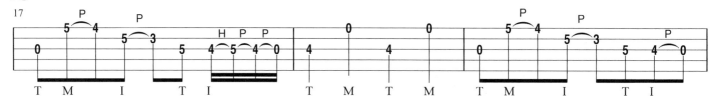

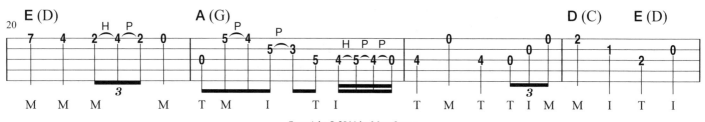

Copyright © 2011 by Mary James
All Rights Reserved   Used by Permission

34

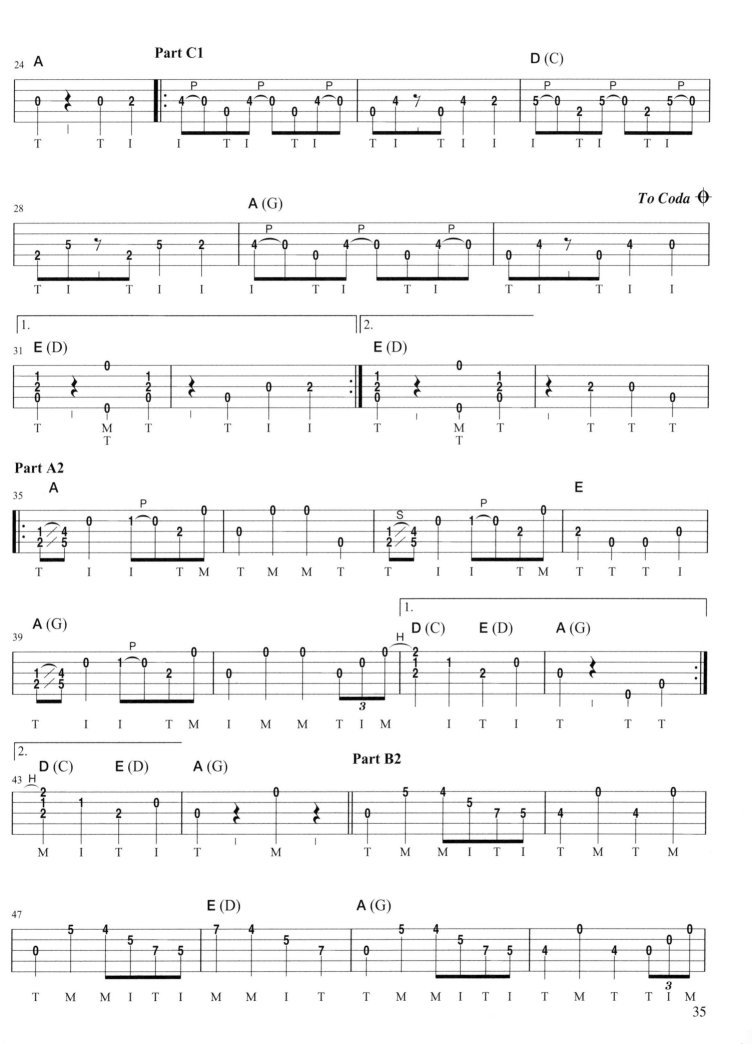

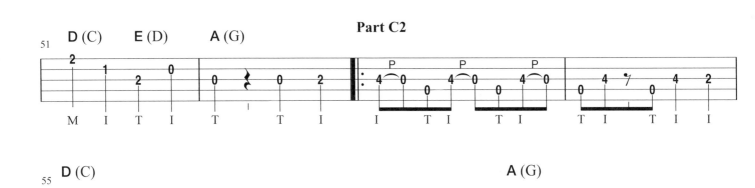
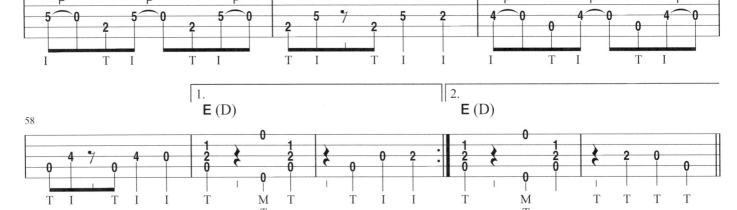
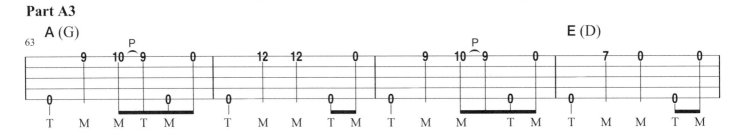
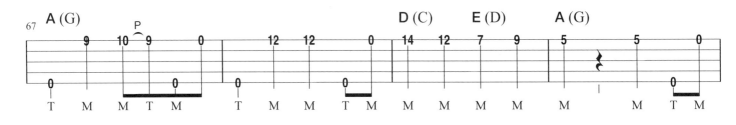
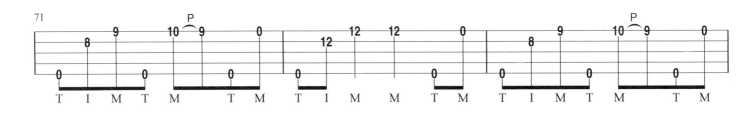
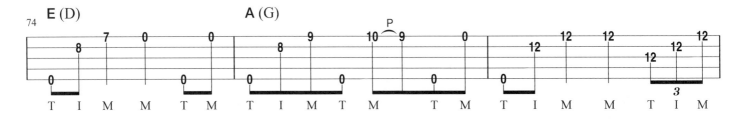

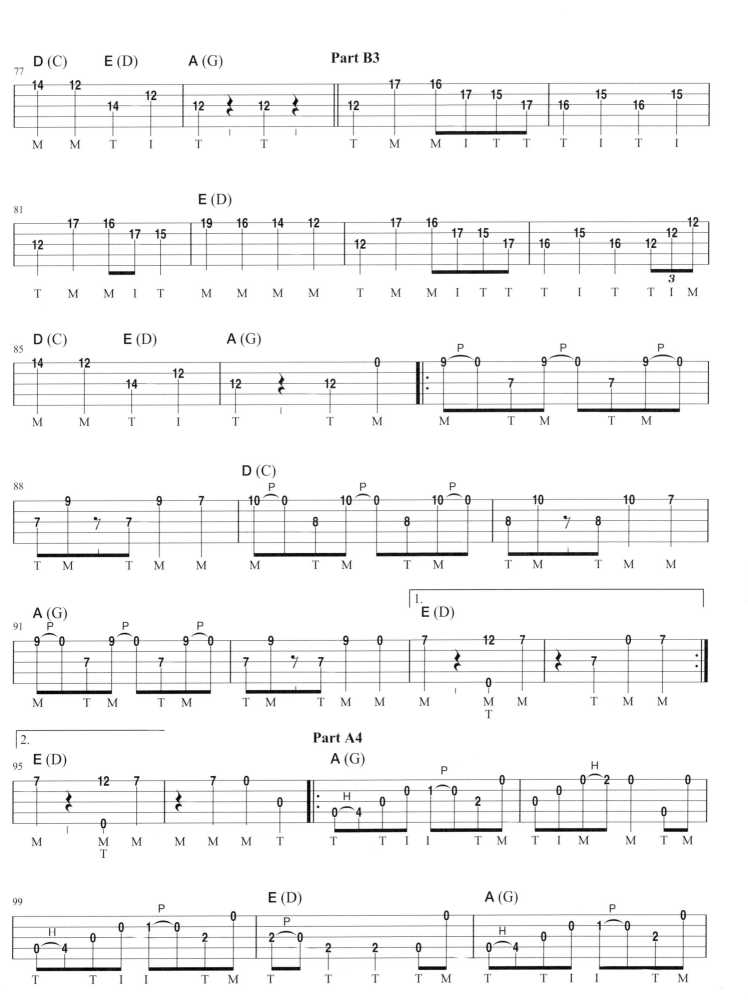

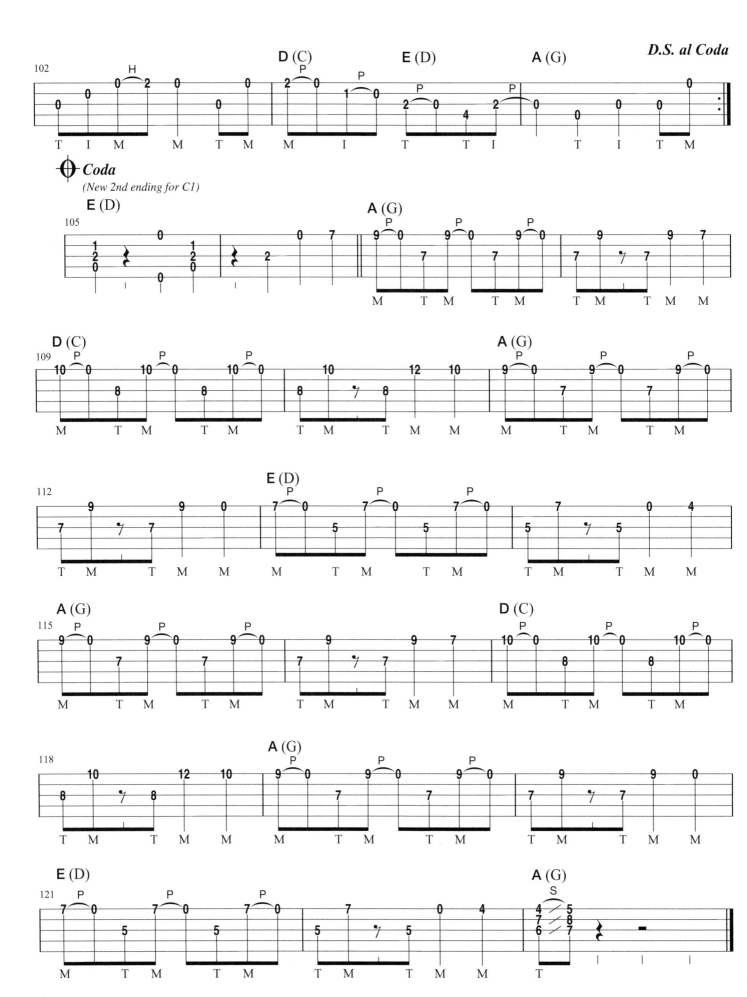

"Off with you! You're a happy fellow, for you'll give happiness and joy to many other people. There is nothing better or greater than that!"
~Ludwig Beethoven

The banjo/guitar duel at the beginning can be played freely. During the guitar's break, you can play your own back-up rolls, chords, or play the deadened-strings, "chucka" rhythm I play on the DVD.

Joy

Written by MARY JAMES and
LUDWIG VAN BEETHOVEN

Key: G

Part "Ode to Joy" 1

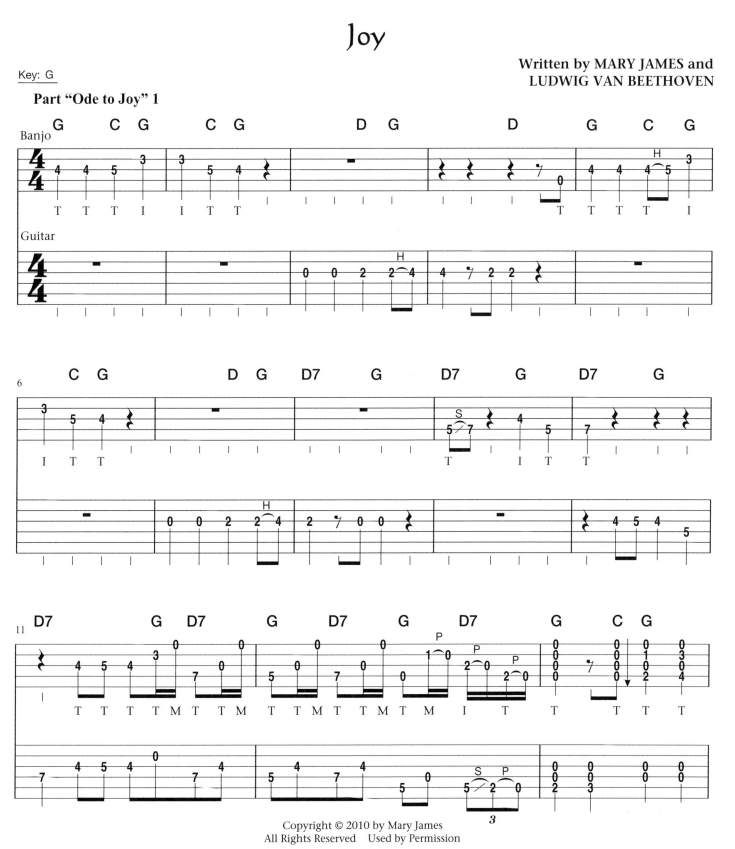

Copyright © 2010 by Mary James
All Rights Reserved   Used by Permission

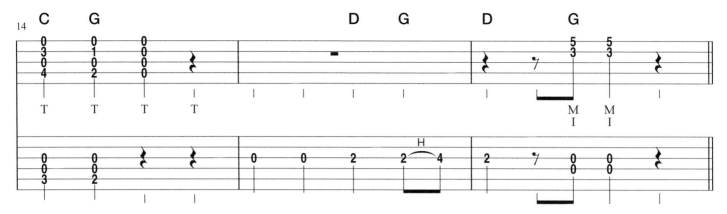

Part A1

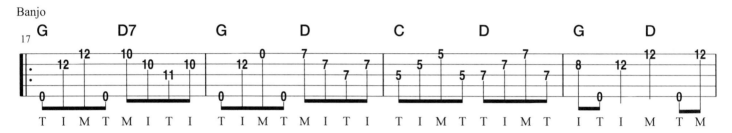

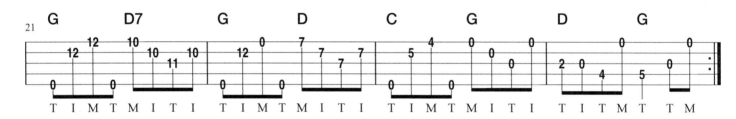

Part B1

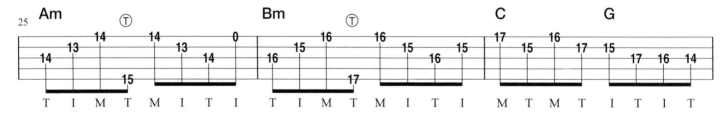

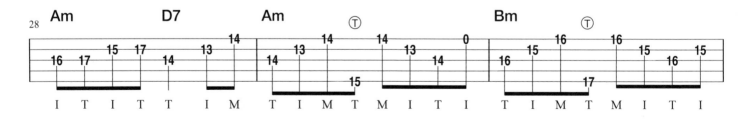

Part C1

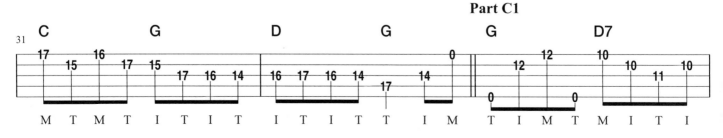

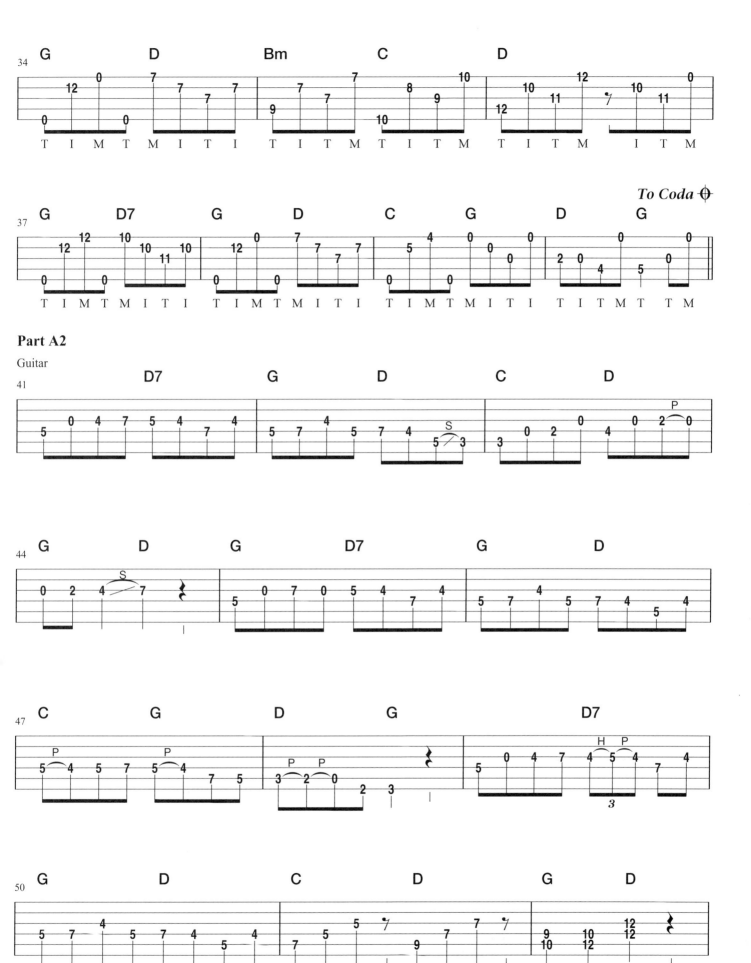

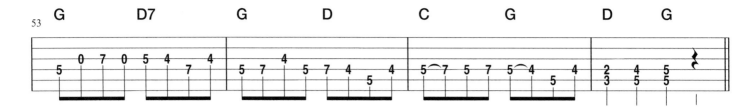

Part B2
Banjo

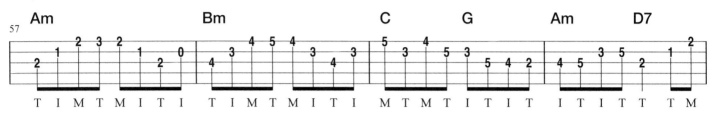

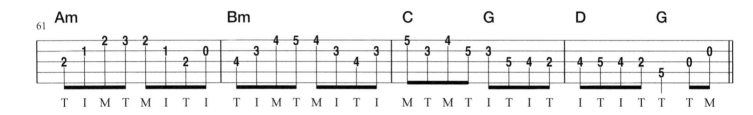

Part C2
Guitar

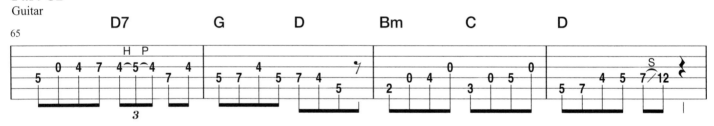

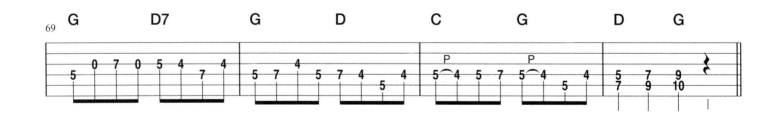

Part "Ode to Joy" 2
Banjo

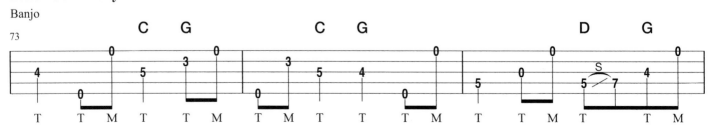

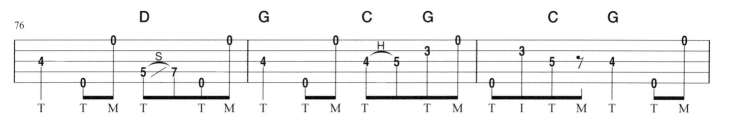
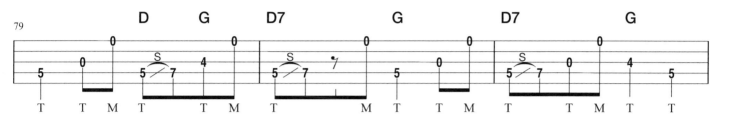
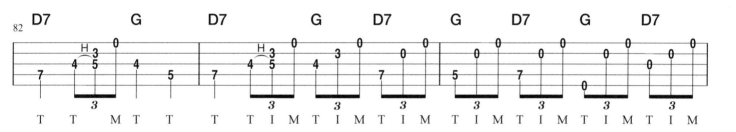
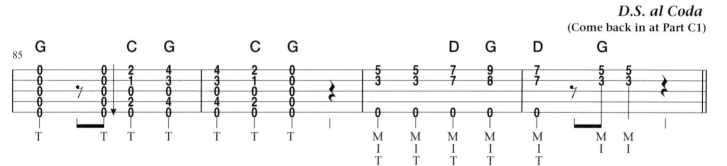
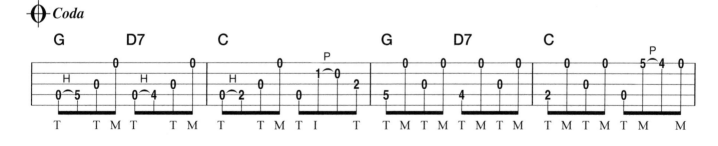
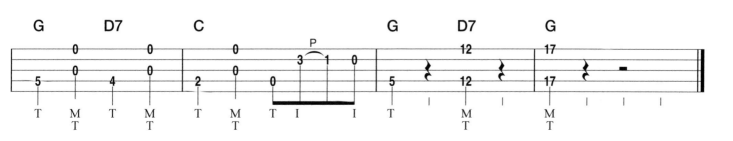

43

The musical genre of this tune is a little hard to explain. The lyrics and banjo notes are very much in sync with each other. Bar 30 starts a string of hammer-ons that are best explained on the DVD. During the chorus, it is best to fret the entire chord as written in the tablature, even though you're not playing all the strings.

Sparrow Alone

Written by
"MEAN" MARY JAMES
and JEAN JAMES

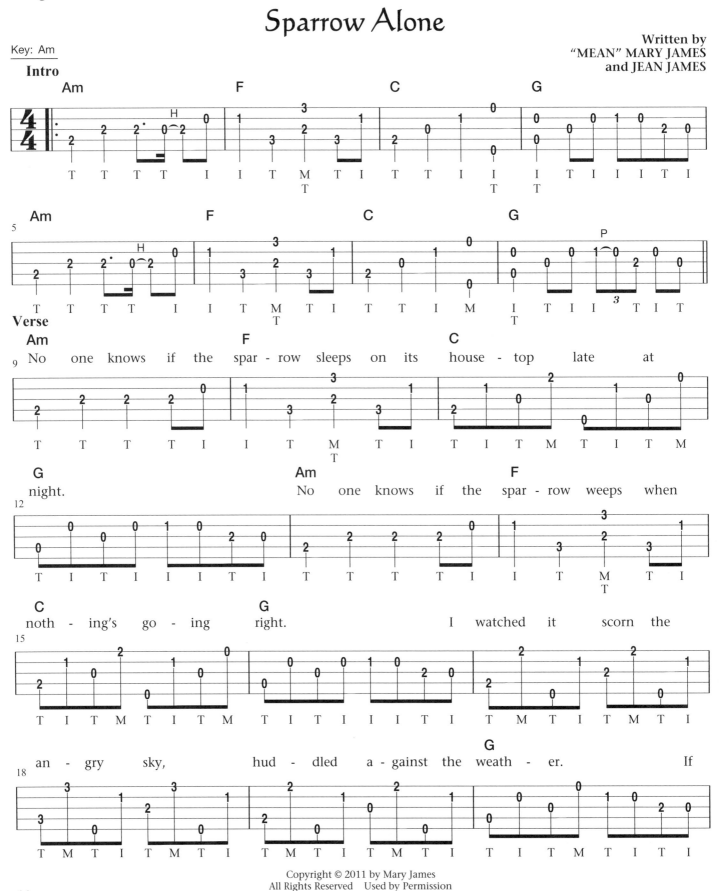

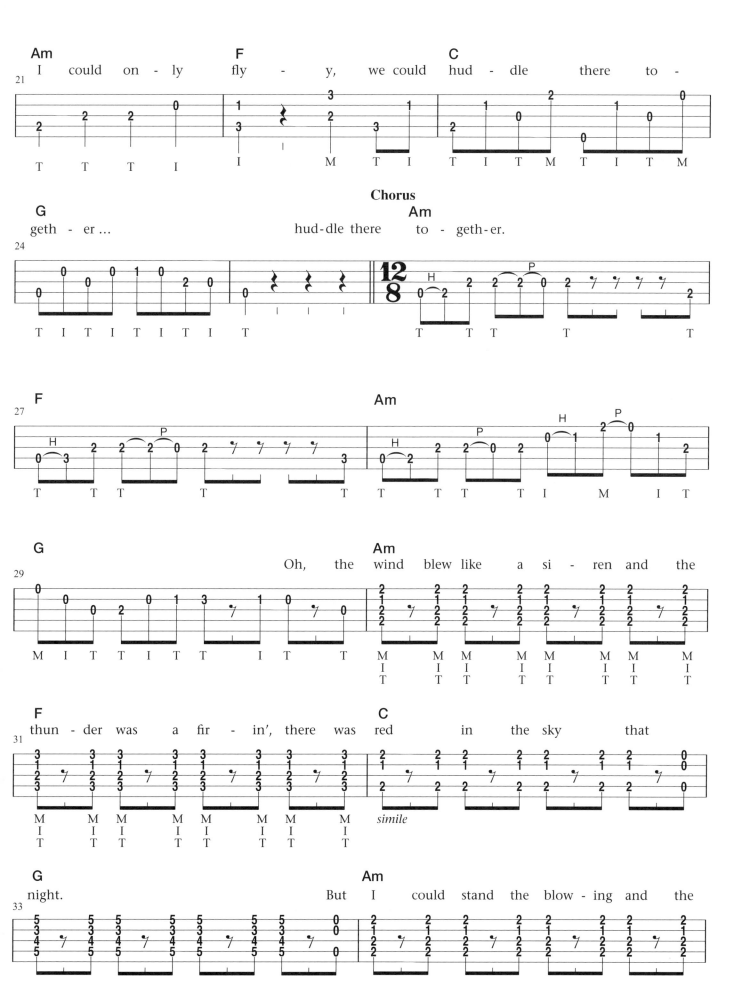

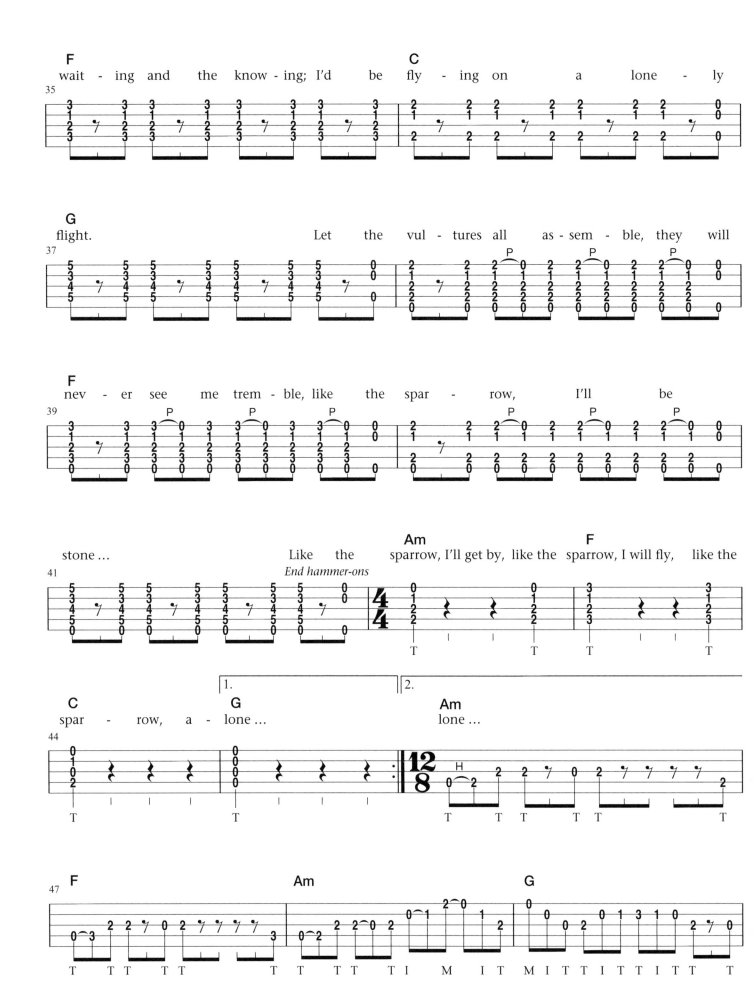

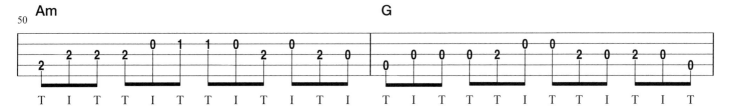
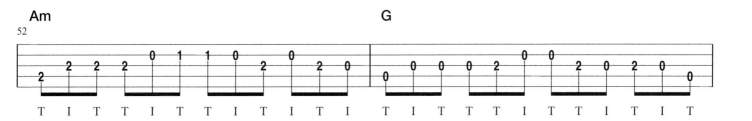
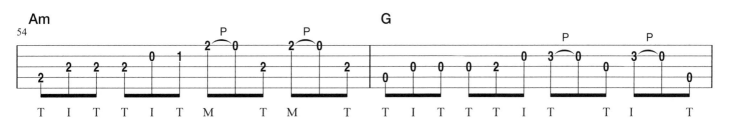
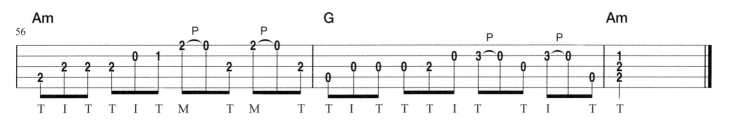

Additional Lyrics

Verse 2: Don't fly into the storm, they said,
but my course was firmly set.
Silently I stared ahead,
a lonely statuette.

I'd seen things no one should see,
I'd faced the great unknown,
like the sparrow I'd fly free
and face the storm alone …
the storm alone.

Chorus: Oh, the wind blew like a siren,
and the thunder was a firin';
there was red in the sky that night.

But I could stand the blowing,
and the waiting and the knowing,
I'd be flying on a lonely flight.

Let the vultures all assemble,
they will never see me tremble,
like the sparrow, I'll be stone.

Like the sparrow, I'll get by,
like the sparrow, I will fly,
like the sparrow, alone …
Sparrow alone.